Happy Ways to Heal the Earth

Gloria Chadwick

Mystical Mindscapes

Books to Enlighten and Empower

Happy Ways to Heal the Earth

Copyright © 1999 by Gloria Chadwick

All rights reserved. No part of this book may be reproduced or utilized in any form or by any means, electronic or mechanical, including photocopying, recording, or by any other information storage and retrieval system, without permission in writing from the publisher, except for brief quotations used in a review.

Publisher's Cataloging-in-Publication Data

Chadwick, Gloria / ISBN 1-883717-22-1
Happy Ways to Heal the Earth
1. Nature 2. Earth 3. Ecology I. Title

Library of Congress Catalog Card Number: 99-93099

Published by Mystical Mindscapes in cooperation with I C.A.R.E. (I Care About the Resources of the Earth) 1908 Cambridge Court, Suite 2A • Palatine, Illinois 60074

Printed in the United States of America by Morris Publishing, Kearney, Nebraska

Books by Gloria Chadwick

Exploring Your Past Lives

Somewhere Over the Rainbow
A Soul's Journey Home

Images and Inner Journeys
Meditations and Visualizations

The Key to Self-Empowerment
Open the Magic Inside Your Mind

Happy Ways to Heal the Earth

Soul Shimmers
Awakening Your Spiritual Self

A Wish, a Hope, and a Prayer

May we all honor and heal the Earth in many happy ways. And may we all, in our own special and joyful ways, be loving caregivers to our Mother Earth.

Acknowledgments

To the people at the Palatine Public Library who began the recycling program there. I don't remember your names but you know who you are.

To all the many writers who have written about ecology and Earth awareness. Thank you for your wonderful books that show your caring and share your knowledge, and inspire us to take care of the Earth.

To all the environmentalists and ecologists in the world who create the groups and organizations to actively help and heal our Earth in so many loving, beautiful ways.

To all the people who take the time every day to recycle and to grow gardens and plant trees, and the many other wonderful things you do. Thank you for caring about our Earth.

To all the publishers who graciously gave me copies of their books that I didn't already have so that I could write a more informative and helpful book for you.

And mostly, thank you to all the nature spirits and flower faeries who whispered in my ear, "Write this book and give it as a gift to the Earth."

Dedication

This book is dedicated to the Earth — a living, breathing, beautiful, vibrant being. Thank you for giving me such a wonderful planet to live on to call my home.

This book is also dedicated to my daughters, Jennifer and Jaime. Thank you Jennifer, for all the rainbows you've given me, and for the garden flowers you gave me every year for Mother's Day. Thank you Jaime, for hugging trees with me, and for loving the Earth as much as I do. Thank you both for all the "upsie" daisies and wonderful wildflowers you brought home for me from your walks through nature.

Contents

I C.A.R.E.

Introduction

Part I — Getting Grounded
1 — Grow a Garden   3
2 — Treasure the Trees   5
3 — Run Through the Rain   7
4 — Take a Wonderful Walk Through Nature   9
5 — Pack a Picnic   11
6 — Earth Day   12
7 — Enjoy the Earth   14
8 — Just Be Happy   16
9 — Tune Into Your True Nature   18

Part II — Appreciate the Animals
10 — Sing to the Birds   23
11 — Share With the Squirrels   26

Part III — Helpful Hints
12 — Remember the R's   31
13 — Carry Canvas   39
14 — Stop Styrofoam   40
15 — Saturday Stuff   42
16 — Share Showers   43
17 — Very Veggie   44

Part IV — A Word of Warning and Healthy Hopes

18 — It's Not Nice to Fool With Mother Nature	47
19 — Playing and Procreating	50
20 — Imagine That... A World View	51

Part V — Garden Glimpses and Tree Tales

21 — Plant With Care	55
22 — Better Than Beans	56
23 — "Love-ins"	58
24 — Joyful Bloomers	60
25 — Digging in the Dirt	61
26 — Flower Power	63
27 — Jungle Joy	64
28 — The Carrot Patch	66
29 — Loving Lure	67
30 — Splash Bash	69
31 — Have You Hugged a Tree Today?	71
32 — Special Trees	73

Part VI — More Than Magical

33 — Breathe	77
34 — Smile at the Sun	78
35 — Promote Peace	79
36 — Whisper to the Wind	81

Part VII — Nature Spirits and Shamans

37 — Make Friends With the Flower Faeries — 85

38 — Shaman's Spirit — 87

Part VIII — Earth Exercises and Explorations

39 — The Earth is Alive — 91

40 — Earth Energies — 94

Part IX — Take Action. Do Something!

41 — Soapbox Stand — 103

42 — Make it Matter — 105

43 — Kids Care — 107

44 — Clean-up Crew — 109

45 — Helping Hands — 112

Part X — Consciously Care

46 — Care About the Earth — 117

Part XI — A Garden of Harmony

47 — A Special Gift From the Earth to You — 121

Publisher's Note — 125

Recommended Reading List — 127

I C.A.R.E.

I C.A.R.E. (I Care About the Resources of the Earth) is a home-grown, garden-variety, not-for-profit organization that was founded in 1989. Its purpose and mission is dedicated and devoted to honoring and healing the Earth.

Some of its many programs include helping to establish recycling centers, facilitating the planting of trees, offering Earth Awareness and Appreciation workshops to raise environmental consciousness, and sharing information and resources with groups of caring people and ecology-centered organizations.

Since its inception, I C.A.R.E. has focused its attention on the local community but has recently begun growing and expanding to encompass the world.

Introduction

Ever since I was a little girl, I knew that the Earth was special, and I treasured her in my heart and with all my heart. I grew my first garden when I was four years old. I planted a few watermelon seeds and they actually GREW! I still remember the joy I felt when I saw the first green shoot coming up out of the Earth. It seemed like a miracle, and was one of the most magical moments in my life. The Earth had given me a gift!

The idea for this book was sown as a seed many years ago when I first began to recycle and thought that perhaps one day I'd write a book about caring for the Earth that offered ways to help and heal the Earth, things like that.

That seed began growing several days before Christmas a year ago when I thought about what I could give to the Earth as a Christmas gift — a love present. I worked on the outline and wrote down my thoughts all day, and scribbled some notes over the next few days. Then I got busy with other books and things, and it sat in my file cabinet for over a year.

The idea budded and came into full bloom in the shower a few weeks ago. I barely had time to get dressed, gulp down a cup of coffee, and turn my computer on to type the words and thoughts that came pouring out of me. Over the next several weeks,

I completely immersed myself in writing this book. I lived, breathed, ate, slept, and dreamed it, and this book is the flower that came to fruition.

I've never written a book this quickly, but the idea grabbed me and just wouldn't let go. The time I spent writing was intense and absolutely joyful. Today is Valentine's Day. How wonderfully magical and appropriate that I finished this book on this day. It truly turned out to be a love present from my heart.

This book is my love present to the Earth and to you. But the book is only a small part of my gift. It's what I do every day to help and heal the Earth — to create a healthy environment and a beautiful place to live in — that's the real gift.

I hope this book will inspire you to help heal the Earth, both for the Earth and for yourself and your children. I hope that my garden stories, and the ideas and suggestions inside this book will encourage you to do the same things I've done and more, in bigger and better ways.

Through your actions, and by your caring, YOU can turn these thoughts and ideas, and your own thoughts and ideas into healing the Earth in many happy ways.

I know that you will find joy many times over in giving to and receiving from the Earth, and in caring for the Earth. Through my words, I've hopefully given you a glimpse into the Earth's soul.

It is my prayer that we all bless the Earth with our love and care, just as she blesses us every day in so many wonderful ways.

Part I

Getting Grounded

Grow a garden and grow yourself.

Hug a tree, plant some trees, and save a tree.

Run through the rain and look for rainbows.

Enjoy the Earth and appreciate the
many gifts that the Earth gives to you.

Take a wonderful walk through nature.

Pack a picnic and eat outside.

Do something special on Earth Day.

Just be happy. Smile.

Tune into your true nature.
Share some good vibrations.

One

Grow a Garden

One of the happiest and most healing things you can do is to grow a garden and tend to it lovingly. It's good for your soul and it's good for the soil.

There's something very special about planting a garden and watching it grow. It's magical and mystical, plus it's just plain fun to play in the dirt, to feel the wonderful, silky touch of the Earth in your hands.

You tend to grow in many wonderful ways — spiritually, emotionally, and mentally — right along with your garden, and you have the added pleasure of knowing that you're helping to create something beautiful that will be treasured by the Earth and enjoyed by many other people.

We often look at the beauty of the Earth and take it for granted that things grow, but really think about it for a few minutes; think about the magic in the Earth that makes this happen.

It's so mysterious, and even a bit mystical, that a tiny, rather nondescript seed can grow into a beautiful, fragrant flower. It's hard to imagine that a little seed has the power within itself, and contains the imprint, to create something so delicate and detailed.

All that the little seed needs is the warm, receptive, nourishing soil of the Earth and the nurturing moisture from the rain to grow. Love and light are vital to its continued growth; the sun provides the light, you provide the love.

It's more than magical when you see that first little green shoot coming up out of the Earth. It gives you so much joy to know that you've helped to make that happen. It's like giving birth. It's a truly awesome experience; it completely opens up your heart with love.

As the flowers grow, bud, and blossom, opening up to you in the warmth and light from the sun, they share their joy at being alive. Grow a garden. You'll be glad you did, and the Earth will love it too.

Two

Treasure the Trees

Trees honor and heal the Earth with their presence. Trees are majestic and magical; they have a soul and life essence that is in complete harmony with the Earth.

You can actually feel the energy and life-source flowing through a tree. The tree is just as much alive as you are. It has an intelligence and an Earth-knowing that it will gladly share with you. A tree offers you much more than shade in the summer; it offers you all the secrets of nature. Sit beneath a tree and meditate. Listen to it whisper to you in your mind and in your heart.

Hug a tree every day. It will make you feel good and the tree will enjoy it too. Trees love to be hugged, to share the harmony of their soul with yours. If you feel uncomfortable hugging trees, then gently touch a tree every time you walk by one.

Plant a tree or two, or maybe three or more in your front and back yards. If you live in an apartment, contact your local park district. Many park districts have forest preserves or nature centers, and can plant a tree for you there or somewhere in your community.

Arrange to have them plant a tree for you and name it after yourself. Visit your tree regularly to hug it and to watch it grow, as it spreads its roots deeply into the richness of the Earth and its branches reach upward to embrace the sky.

Or give a tree as a gift. Have the tree planted in a friend's name; send them a picture of it and a gift card, telling them where their tree is located.

Another very happy and healing thing you can do is to save a tree every year. Buy a fake tree at Christmas. This honors the Earth and shows that you care.

Three

Run Through the Rain

Remember when you were a little child and you ran through the rain, loving the soft kisses of the raindrops on your face and skin? Remember how you used to splash in the mud puddles with carefree abandon and total happiness? Remember how you used to dance around in circles, with your arms wide open to embrace the sky, raising your face up and sticking out your tongue to catch the raindrops? Remember the sheer delight and pure joy you felt inside you?

Now that you're all grown up, you walk slowly through the rain with an umbrella to protect you. You pull your raincoat tightly around you, afraid that you'll get wet. And then you complain about the weather!

When the sun comes out after the rain, chances are that you don't even notice the beautiful rainbow because you're either too busy to look up at the sky or you're inside. How dull and dreary!

The weather is wonderful. Toss your umbrella and your negative thoughts. Run joyfully through the rain again, no matter how old you are now.

The next time it rains, jump for joy. Take your shoes off and run through the rain. Squish the mud between your toes. Splash in the puddles. Catch the raindrops on your tongue and taste their delicious wetness. Be free and happy. As the rain nourishes the Earth, let it also nourish your heart and soul.

When the sun comes out, look up at the sky for a shimmering rainbow. Feel the awe and wonder and beauty of it inside your soul. Then look around you at the wet, beautiful Earth and notice all the sparkling rainbows dancing on the leaves of the bushes and the petals of the flowers.

Breathe deeply and smell the wonderful scent of the wet Earth, freshly nourished and cleansed by the rain. Tune into all these wondrous things around you. Bring them inside you, and feel the joy and harmony of them within your heart.

The Earth has just blessed you with a beautiful gift. Treasure it, and thank her for it. Your appreciation and enjoyment of the rain and the rainbow is very happy and healing for the Earth. Honor her with your gratitude, and have fun running through the rain!

Four

Take a Wonderful Walk Through Nature

Every time you take a walk through nature and notice a beautiful flower, or touch a tree, or appreciate the natural wonder and beauty of the Earth, you honor and heal the Earth.

Go for a leisurely walk. Take some time to be in nature, and to enjoy the Earth. Walk on the Earth just to walk — to feel connected and grounded with the Earth. This returns you to your natural state of being.

Take your shoes off and walk barefoot in the grass. Feel the rich, velvety softness of the cool, green grass on your bare feet. The Earth will love your touch, and you can feel the love and energy emanating through the ground, radiating upward from the Earth to you.

This is one of the many ways you can communicate with the Earth, to attune yourself to her life-force and energy, and to share your life-force and energy with her.

Take a walk through a nature preserve or a forest to appreciate and enjoy the natural, pristine beauty of the Earth, to see the Earth in her most natural and beautiful form.

Let this wonderful walk through nature inspire you to help return her to perfect health and harmony. Allow yourself to connect with nature, to replenish yourself and to share yourself with the Earth, just as she shares herself with you. The Earth appreciates your companionship.

Five

Pack a Picnic

When the weather is warm, eat your lunch outside, either alone or with a friend. If you work in an office, this gives you special time away to relax and refresh yourself, to enjoy the wonderful weather and the sunshine.

Being outside can brighten up a bad day, and gets you away from the (sometimes nasty and negative) people in the office. It reduces stress, and you can share your lunch with the birds and with the Earth.

If you're a stay-at-home mom or dad, pack a picnic, and enjoy the Earth and the warmth of the weather with your kids. If you, or they, are sloppy eaters, and you drop your food on the ground, the Earth will be happy to compost it for you.

When you're finished eating, you can work off the calories by chasing after your children, who probably won't sit still once they're done eating, or by walking or jogging back to the office. The fresh air is beneficial for you, and, as a special treat or dessert, you get to feel grounded to the Earth.

Six

Earth Day

April 22nd is Earth Day — a very special day dedicated to the Earth. Do something special on this day. Commemorate it in a sacred way.

Go to a nursery and buy flower seeds or bedding plants, or bushes and trees.

Plan your garden in your mind, or if the Earth is warm and ready, begin planting it.

Breathe the fresh air.

Dance in the sunshine.

Sing to the soil.

Smell the flowers.

Hug a tree.

Play in the dirt.

Plant a rosebush.

Smile at the sky.

Run through a meadow.

Sit on the Earth to feel grounded and to connect your soul with hers.

Make a wish on a cloud.

Put a flower in your hair.

Just be happy.

Enjoy the beauty of the Earth.

Feel harmony inside your heart.

Talk to the flower faeries.

Whisper to the wind.

Meditate in the woods.

Wade in a babbling brook.

Walk barefoot through the grass.

Climb a mountain.

Give your neighbors a flower.

Honor the Earth. Give her a gift — a love present — on her special day.

Do whatever you want in the way that you want to do it — a happy way that you feel will be helpful and healing for the Earth.

Seven

Enjoy the Earth

Take a moment every now and then to be grateful to the Earth, to appreciate her, and to thank her for your beautiful home. The Earth will hear you and will respond to your love with feelings of appreciation. The Earth will thank you by giving you many gifts and magical moments of being in nature in return.

Be open to receiving the gifts given lovingly to you from the Earth. All of her gifts are natural and are given freely for you to enjoy.

Some of her many gifts include the sun and the rain, a beautiful, fragrant flower that catches your attention and brings you pleasure, the forests and trees that offer you mystical moments of meditation and solitude, and the majesty of a mountain that reaches up into the sky.

A quiet walk along the beach offers you peacefulness and serenity as you listen to the gentle ebb and flow of the waves. The sound and motion of the waves matches your inner rhythm. Watching the waves at the beach puts you in rhythm and in tune with yourself and the Earth.

A rainbow, shimmering and sparkling in the sky inspires a sense of awe and wonder and joy inside you. It's a very beautiful gift from the Earth to you that offers you magical moments. The next time you see a rainbow, stop and take the time to really see it and enjoy it, to respect the wonderful beauty of it, and to fully admire and appreciate it.

The Earth's most precious gift to us is the land to live on, a beautiful, happy place to call our home. Let's keep her alive and healthy. It's our most precious gift to her.

Eight

Just Be Happy

That's all you have to do. Just be happy. The Earth will feel and sense your happiness and will be happy too. This is one of the easiest and most effective ways to honor and heal the Earth. So just be happy. Smile, and share your happiness with the Earth.

You might think that this is too easy and wonder how it can be such an effective way to heal the Earth. It's a good question that you can answer for yourself. Just think about it for a minute or two before you read the next paragraph.

When you're with a happy person, how do you feel? Happy! You don't even have to be near someone who is happy to sense their vibes and to feel happy, too. Just by thinking about them, you feel happy.

Every living thing radiates and emanates energy, and that energy affects everyone and everything. By just being happy, you're emanating and radiating good vibes and joy in your thoughts and feelings, affecting other people, and the Earth in a happy, healing way.

    Send good thoughts to the Earth every day. Spread a lot of good feelings of cheer and joy. Your joy is wonderfully powerful and goes a long way. Smile and just be happy!

Nine

Tune Into Your True Nature

Have you ever wondered why you feel so peaceful when you're in nature — in a beautiful garden or walking through the woods, or in any other natural, outside setting? Why does being at a beach and listening to the waves as they gently ebb and flow relax and soothe you? Why does being near a powerful waterfall gushing down a mountainside fill you with an exhilarating feeling of energy?

Because the Earth is naturally peaceful, relaxing, soothing, and at times exhilarating, exciting, and powerful. The Earth has the same vibrations and feelings that we have. Our true inner nature matches the calm, happy vibrations of the Earth. When we tune into the natural vibrations of the Earth, we return to our naturalness.

Have you ever wondered why, when you're feeling stressed out or angry, or sad or depressed, if you can be in nature, you immediately feel relaxed, calm, and happier? Because the Earth has wonderful healing energies and shares those vibrations with you.

Have you ever noticed that when you're outside on a beautiful sunny day, you feel happy and have more energy? Do you know why the season of Spring brings forth feelings of vitality, of renewal and rejuvenation inside you? Because the Earth is bursting forth with life and energy, and shares those feelings with you.

The Earth is a living, vibrant being with a soul, just like us. Why does seeing a beautiful rainbow, or a brilliant sunrise or a golden sunset, inspire feelings of awe, wonder, joy, and reverence inside you? Because the sun radiates both energy and light, and those vibrations are in harmony with our spiritual nature. The vibrations of a rainbow match the vibrations of our soul.

We can share our natural vibrations with the Earth to help heal her. The Earth gives us many happy, healing gifts if we will simply accept them and appreciate them, if we will just be in nature and in harmony with the Earth and in tune with ourselves.

The Earth offers us the opportunity to tune into our natural state of being — one of peace, health, and happiness. We can do the same for the Earth. Tune into your true nature and share your good vibrations with the Earth.

Part II

Appreciate the Animals

Sing to the birds.
Serenade them with a song.
Listen to their cheerful chirps.

Share with the squirrels.
These cute little creatures — in their
own way — help you grow your garden.

Ten

Sing to the Birds

Serenade the birds with a song. They serenade you all the time. You wake up to their cheerful chirps outside your bedroom window in the morning. The birds sing at sunrise, welcoming in the dawn — the new day — with a happy song and harmony, inviting you to rise and share the light.

The rhythm and sound of their songs change during the day. The tone and vibration are different in the afternoon. They tend to chatter, socializing with you and with each other.

You listen to them joyfully sing to each other in the trees during the day. It seems that sunshine and light makes them happy, or maybe they're communicating with the sun, or with the flowers and trees and the Earth, sharing their joy. When you sing in the sun, they'll come and listen to you and share their songs, gathering in your garden.

At night, their songs change again. They're softer and the rhythm is slower, with longer, lower tones. Their songs are mellow and melodious, inviting the gentle moonlight and the stars into the sky. They sing a sweet, soothing, loving lullaby — singing you and the Earth, and each other peacefully into sleep.

The weather also orchestrates their songs. They sing more in the warmth and brightness of the sunshine. On cold, gray, cloudy days, they huddle and hum to one another in soft, cozy, comforting tones. The vibrations of their songs are similar to how you feel being inside on a very rainy or stormy day.

They're tuned into the rhythms of nature, into the flow of energies and cycles and patterns of the Earth. Their songs change with the seasons. Spring is a time when they'll burst forth with song, heralding in the new buds on the flowers, bushes, and trees, encouraging and inviting them to grow — announcing their arrival and asking you to notice the buds and flowers, and to admire them. During the summer, they sing jubilantly all day long, sharing their joy with the flowers.

In the fall, their songs have a sad tone and quality, saying good-bye to their dear summer friends — the leaves and the flowers. In the winter, if they stay, they tend to hibernate in their nests and you don't hear them often, but most go south for the warmth of the sun.

They sing their soul to you, sharing the harmony inside their heart, and they love listening to you and talking with you. Music and sound are a universal language. While they may not understand the words in your song or your speech, just as you may not understand theirs, they do understand the music and the tone.

Birds — like all animals and living things — are

very aware of and sensitive to your unspoken feelings. They can communicate through their body postures, just as we do with one another, through the tilt of their head, the look in their eyes, and the way they stand or move about.

They're also well versed in the silent language of thought. They hear and respond to the energy vibrations of unspoken thoughts. If you're tuned into them, you can receive their thoughts telepathically. (Have you ever noticed that they particularly like to perch on telephone wires? It could be that this is symbolic!)

It's easy and fun to communicate with them. They respond well to your laughter, light-hearted conversation, and happy, humming sounds. The songs you sing to them, and to the Earth, will attract them into your garden and create vibrations of happiness and joy.

The rhythm, the tone, your voice, the vibration of the melody and the tune of your song opens your heart and shares your happy feelings with the birds and with the Earth.

A special benefit of singing to the birds is that it will help to nourish your garden as well as helping it to grow bigger and better. As you attract more birds to listen to you serenade them, and invite them to sing to you, they'll give you many gifts of bird droppings to fertilize the soil.

Sing a happy song every now and then. Hum a tune, and be in rhythm and harmony with the Earth.

Eleven

Share With the Squirrels

The squirrels who live in my neighborhood can be quite pesky and persistent! When I first began growing my vegetable and flower gardens, the squirrels would constantly eat my tomatoes, cucumbers, broccoli, and green peppers, and they'd bite off the buds of my rhododendron, hibiscus, and rose bushes, hiding them in secret places in the Earth.

It seems that they were determined to eat all my vegetables, and every bud that grew on my bushes before they had a chance to bloom. They also had a definite interest in and a perpetual habit of digging up the flower beds to hide their treasures in.

It became a daily ritual to swear at the squirrels and try to scare them away by verbally threatening them and brandishing a nasty-looking garden utensil in their direction, which mildly amused them. They'd look at me with a quizzical look in their eyes trying to figure out what this crazy lady was doing.

They'd stand their ground, sitting on their hind

legs with their front paws together in front of them as if they were either praying or begging me for food. I'd end up laughing at them because they looked so silly and cute, then chase them away when the verbal abuse and threatening measures didn't work.

After aggravating me for weeks, I began to realize that they had just as much right to the vegetables and flowers as I did. Plus, they were helping to seed and grow gardens by planting their pilferings in the Earth.

It's simply their nature to hide their food in the ground, then dig up their food cache when they're hungry, and being the forgetful little creatures that they are, they were actually growing gardens too, by not remembering where they stashed their food. I just didn't like that they were doing their grocery shopping in my garden.

Searching for solutions to this problem, I came up with a plan. I thought about how I could work in harmony with them to share the land. I thought that if I respected them, they would respect me. I decided to make a deal with them, to give them their own special space in my garden.

I talked to them and told them what my plans were, and asked for their cooperation. They seemed to be agreeable to the idea — they listened to me and looked at me pleasantly — so I planted a little vegetable garden for them, showed them where it was, and gave them permission to eat and enjoy to their heart's content. I asked them to leave the rest of the garden for me. Surprisingly, it worked fairly well but their memory does elude them from time to time.

I wish the squirrels would be a little more cooperative and a lot more perceptive. It seems they have some difficulty recognizing the difference between their territory and mine.

But they're cute, and I've learned to live with them peacefully. Now the squirrels and I grow gardens together.

Part III

Helpful Hints

Recycle, reduce, and reuse.
Reducing recipes for your kitchen.

Do Saturday stuff with a friend.
Share errands and save gas.

Carry canvas to show that you care.

Share a shower to save water.

Stop styrofoam from spreading.

Go organic and grow veggie.

Twelve

Remember the R's

Doing the three R's — recycling, reducing, and reusing — on a day-to-day basis is good for both the Earth and you. It takes only a little bit of common sense and a lot of caring all the time.

You're not in school anymore and the three R's — Reading, Writing, and Arithmetic — have changed, but life itself is a school and the Earth is your classroom. Since I'm a teacher, here are some life-long homework assignments for you:

Recycle

In addition to the regular recycling of newspapers, plastic bags, bottles, and aluminum cans, originate innovative ways to recycle whatever you can. Be creative, conscious, and caring.

Think about the things that you use and find ways to recycle them that are new or different. Improvise and individualize, depending on your special uniqueness and interests, and what you do for work.

Don't ignore the obvious. I'm a writer, so I make

sure my publisher prints all my books on recycled paper. It's a deal-breaker in my contract. I self-publish some of my books and always print them on recycled paper. It costs a bit more but it's well worth it. It makes me happy to save trees, and the Earth appreciates it too.

Homework Assignment #1 — Write down thirty ways you can recycle items that you use every day. Then recycle them, and continue to find more ways. Talk to other people. Encourage them to recycle.

Reduce

In addition to reducing your use of the Earth's resources, such as running errands with a friend or car pooling to save gas, reduce your consumption of non-renewable sources of energy by turning off the lights when you leave a room.

Let's put a little light on the subject of lights. Halogen light bulbs cost more than regular light bulbs, but last longer and are very energy-efficient. In the long run, you save more money and energy when you use them. Brighten up your home, and lighten up on the energy load.

Look for ways to reduce in your work. I use both sides of the paper when I write, then recycle the paper. When I print out my draft manuscripts, I use one-and-a-half spacing instead of double spacing. I invariably save a page or two for every chapter and still have lots of room to scribble between the lines. I've saved reams of paper this way, and lots of money at the same time. I've also saved a few trees in the process.

Don't go kitchen crazy. This is one of the most wasted-energy usage areas in your home. Learn how to be a creative cook and a gourmet energy-saver. Here are a few reducing recipes:

- When you're cooking something in the oven that only needs ten minutes to finish cooking, turn the oven off. There's plenty of heat in there to finish cooking your food.

- Instead of using several pans and burners on the stove, use only one. One of my favorite dinners is ham, potatoes, and brussel sprouts. Instead of running my ham around in the microwave, steaming my sprouts, and boiling my potatoes separately, I cook them together. They get all mixed up together in your stomach anyway.

This turned out to be yummy good, because everything flavored everything else, and I only had one pan to wash. Cook stews, soups, and casseroles more frequently. Combine ingredients.

- When you're cooking something stinky, like broccoli or fish, instead of turning on the exhaust fan or spraying an air freshener to get rid of the smell, light a scented candle.

- Save water and energy: don't run the dishwasher half full. Ditto for the washing machine and dryer.

Homework Assignment #2 — Write down thirty ways you can reduce what you use every day. Then either eliminate them or lessen your usage, and continue to find more ways.

Reuse

Ask yourself if you really *need* all the stuff that you only use once and then throw away. My mom would always tell me, "Waste not, want not." I'm sure your mom told you the same thing. These are wise words, and very true. Reducing and reusing comes naturally to most people and is also economical.

Think twice before you throw away your stuff. What can you recycle? What can you reuse? What could someone else use and appreciate? Perhaps you can give your old clothes that are still in good condition, and other household items that you no longer want or need, to GoodWill or donate them to a resale shop that serves a charitable organization.

There are so many simple things that are right in front of our faces that we don't see them. For instance, instead of buying plastic containers to store left-over food in, use the plastic tubs of butter and the plastic containers for salads and dips from the deli to put your left-overs in.

Reuse the plastic bags from grocery stores and other stores to put your garbage in, or take the bags back to the store and use them a second time. Many stores, especially health food stores, will give you a nickel for every plastic bag you reuse in this manner. If you don't want to use them a second time, many stores have a recycling bin especially for plastic bags. Put them there.

Instead of recycling or reusing plastic bags, don't use them at all. Use a canvas bag for your groceries and your other shopping.

Buy your fruits and vegetables loose, instead of putting them into plastic bags. This works well with larger fruits and vegetables that have their own skin. While this may be aggravating to the check-out clerk, you're saving plastic. Smile nicely at him or her and explain that you care about the Earth.

What you think of as trash can actually be a work of art. A tin can and some popsicle sticks, with a little glue and imagination, becomes a beautiful pencil holder. (I had help with this idea. My daughter, Jennifer, made this for me when she was in kindergarten for a Mother's Day present.)

I had an old barbecue grill. Someone had stolen the lid and one of the racks was missing. Instead of throwing it in the trash, I filled it with dirt and planted flowers in it.

Homework Assignment #3 — Write down thirty ways you can reuse everything. Look at what you use, see how these items can be reused, then reuse them. Find ways to improvise and to be more creative with what you have. Use only what you need and don't overuse.

Respect

While we're on the subject of recycling, reducing, and reusing, let's add another "R" — Respect.

Respect the Earth every day, in everything that you do, and in every way that you can. This is so easy to accomplish. Simply consciously care. That's all there is to it and this is what respect is all about.

Homework Assignment #4 — Think twice about things that might bring harm to the Earth and don't do them. Come up with 101 creative, innovative ways to help the Earth.

There are more R's that are respectful, and helpful and healing, that we can all do.

Replenish and Restore

Give back what you take. If we continue to drain the Earth, soon we won't have anything left to take. We'll deplete the Earth of all her resources, and she'll have nothing left to give.

Make conscious choices when you shop. Buy products without packaging or with minimal packaging that you can easily recycle. Buy in bulk when you can; this also eliminates extra packaging. Choose products that are environmentally friendly.

Homework Assignment #5 — Give more than you take. Make it a goal every day to give something back. Make it relative and proportionate to what you take. Don't limit yourself to merely replacing. Replenish things before you take them. Restore everything you can. This gifts both the Earth and you, and assures an ample supply.

Renew and Rejuvenate

Just as we need sleep to renew and rejuvenate ourselves, so does the Earth. Give her a nice, healthy rest to refresh herself. She needs her beauty sleep too.

Give her some breathing room. Let her be in her own sacred spaces by herself. How would you like it if someone was constantly hovering around you, using and abusing you, and walking all over you?

Leave the Earth's natural areas alone, and let her run wild. Give her the freedom and independence she deserves. These are her special places, where she can just be herself without us bothering her all the time or building things on what we mistakenly think of as unused spaces.

Let the Earth take care of her natural areas in her own way. She's very wise and quite independent. Actually, she doesn't need us at all; she's being very nice by letting us live on her and take from her.

Don't try to help her when she doesn't need our help. Sometimes what we think of as help is interference. Don't rake the leaves; let them return to the Earth to nourish the soil and to blanket the little seeds that are close to the surface, to keep them warm and safe during the winter.

A dead, rotting tree is home to lots of her little friends, like the insects. Let her have her very special friends — the birds, the animals, and the many others that she gives a home to and shares her life with. They are just as important as we are.

In fact, they're much more Earth-conscious than we are. They take only what they need from the Earth and replenish her in many ways. They instinctively know so much more about nature and ecology than we do. Maybe we could learn a lot by simply observing nature, by watching the Earth in her natural environment.

Homework Assignment #6 — Appreciate the

Earth; don't abuse her. Treat her with love and respect. Honor her.

Remember the Reasons

There are so many reasons to help the Earth that will benefit both the Earth and us in many wonderful ways. Think twice about what you do before you do it. Think about how it will affect and impact the Earth. Simply by giving careful thought to everything that we do, and by taking conscious, caring actions, we can heal our Earth.

Homework Assignment #7 — Remember to recycle, reduce, and reuse all the time, in every way that you can. Remember to respect, replenish, restore, renew, and rejuvenate the Earth every day.

Thirteen

Carry Canvas

Use canvas tote bags for your groceries and the other shopping that you do, rather than using paper or plastic bags. For women: If you're purchasing a small item, tell the check-out clerk that you don't need a bag. Put the item, along with the receipt, in your purse. Carry a canvas bag to work with all the stuff you need — your sweater, your lunch, a good book to read, whatever.

If someone accuses you of being a bag lady, tell him or her that you care about the Earth and that you're helping to save the Earth's resources. Maybe you'll inspire that person to be a bag lady too.

It seems that most men are embarrassed to carry a canvas bag. They prefer to be macho and lug all their stuff around without a bag. Take pity on them; they haven't learned to do things the easy way yet. But some men are wise enough to cram all their stuff into a briefcase or a sports bag.

Carrying canvas saves paper and plastic bags, and shows that you care. It silently shares your message, especially if it has an Earth-oriented design. It's an easy way to honor and heal the Earth.

Fourteen

Stop Styrofoam

It's growing and breeding everywhere. It's like putting a girl and boy rabbit together in the same cage but unlike the rabbits, styrofoam doesn't fertilize the Earth with its droppings. Stop styrofoam dead in its tracks before it gets out of hand.

Buy your burgers at fast food restaurants wrapped in paper or foil. Talk to the managers whose restaurants use styrofoam. Tell them that you like their food, and would buy it more often if they'd use paper or foil. If you're going to eat inside instead of doing the drive-through, have them wrap your burger in a napkin.

If you think you'll probably be doing a doggy bag when you go out for dinner, bring a zip-lock baggie or a plastic container with you for your left-overs, rather than having the server put them in a styrofoam container.

If you buy your coffee to go on the mad rush to work in the morning, use pre-made plastic cups with a handle and lid that you can carry in your car and reuse.

Bring your own coffee mug to work to drink your tea or coffee instead of using styrofoam cups. Every time you use your mug, you'll be helping to heal the Earth and you'll also be showing your co-workers that you care.

A possible fringe benefit to this is that you can tell your boss that you're saving the company money because you're not using their styrofoam cups. Then ask for a raise.

Fifteen

Saturday Stuff

Share your Saturday stuff. Combine your errands and go grocery shopping with a friend. This takes the drudge out of your errands; it also saves gas and gives you the pleasure of your friend's company.

Do a leisurely lunch together. Take some time to enjoy life and to relax. You probably have the day off from work. Celebrate your freedom while you accomplish your errands.

If you live close to the store and can walk to do your errands, then take a walk or ride your bike. This also saves gas and gives you great exercise.

While you're outside running your errands, take a few moments to look around you at the Earth to recognize and appreciate what a wonderful world you live in.

Sixteen

Share Showers

Share a shower with a live-in lover, your spouse, or your small children. It saves both time and water, and you have someone to scrub your back. It can also improve your relationship with your shower-sharer.

Brush your teeth with all of the above people. There's something about spitting in the same sink that brings you closer together and forms a bond. In addition, you can play spitting games. See if you can get your hand out of the way before the other person spits on it.

While we're on the subject of sink-spitting and shower-sharing, here's a helpful hint: Install low-flow aerators in your shower head and sink faucet. This saves even more water and you and your partner will never miss it.

I wouldn't advise any kind of tandem-toilet thing, but you can get the porcelain god into the picture. Before you sit on your throne the next time, put a brick into the tank. Every time you flush, you'll save water.

Seventeen

Very Veggie

Grow a vegetable garden in your back yard or on your patio or balcony. It's easy and fun to do, and most veggies require very little work. They're rapid growers and tend to proliferate. Many vegetables grow as vines and take only a small space.

If you don't have the space or a place to grow your own, buy organically-grown veggies at a health food store. They taste delicious and are free from pesticides. They're healthier for you and are grown in an environment that honors and heals the Earth.

They may cost a little more but they're well worth the price, both in terms of nutrition and taste, and in ways of caring for the Earth.

Part IV

A Word of Warning and Healthy Hopes

It's not nice to fool with Mother Nature; you could get into very serious trouble and have to pay the consequences.

Take procreation, co-creating, and rebirthing to a higher level of respect and caring.

Imagine that the world is a peaceful, happy, beautiful place to live.

Eighteen

It's Not Nice to Fool With Mother Nature

Through our thoughtlessness and carelessness, and our lack of foresightedness, we've been destroying our Earth. We've been harming the Earth in many terrible, hurting ways, and we need to change what we've been doing. We need to undo the harm we've done and to heal her.

We are the fools to damage the Earth, to wreak havoc and destruction to our beautiful home. We have debilitated and depleted her. We need to find and employ ways to become more conscious and wiser, to create harmony and to re-build our Earth into the garden she once was.

Before you litter — before you toss your trash on the Earth — think about how it will affect and impact nature and the balance of ecology. Think about what you're doing to the landscape and to the environment.

Think about how you'd feel if someone was tossing their trash at you, or dumping it on your front yard or inside your home. Be respectful of the Earth, and of the beauty of the land. Toss your trash where it belongs — in the garbage dumpster.

While we're on the subject of trash, let's get toxic. How would you feel if someone was putting unhealthy, harmful chemicals into your body and into the air you breathe, and the water you drink? You'd probably get sick and vomit. Let me tell you the truth. You and I, and the Earth, are being poisoned.

Someone really is putting putrid pesticides into you, but not enough to make you vomit — yet! These toxic chemicals certainly aren't healthy for you, but you ingest them every time you eat the commercially-grown fruits and vegetables that are supposed to be healthy for you.

In addition, the grains that are processed into breads and cereals contain chemicals and pesticides. Even meats and poultry have them because the animals graze the land which has been sprayed and saturated with pesticides.

Many industries make it a common practice to dump their toxic wastes and harmful chemicals into lakes and rivers, and both into and on the land. Traces of these chemicals are in our drinking water.

This makes me sick just thinking about it, and it should make all of us scared and sick enough to do something about it — to stop it and to find Earth-honoring ways to grow our food and dispose of toxic wastes safely.

All of us, and the Earth, are becoming sick because of it, but what choice does the Earth have?

We're the ones dumping on her and in her. We have a choice; we can grow our own organic vegetable gardens or buy our fruits and grains that are grown naturally and pesticide-free at a health food store. Let's be more healing, and less harmful, both for ourselves and for the Earth.

The Earth is very sick. She is dying, slowly and painfully, a tortuous, agonizing death. If she dies, we will too. We won't have a land suitable enough to sustain us and to live on. I hope this sad truth — this very real fact — scares you enough to do something about it **NOW**.

The Earth wants to heal herself, and is trying to heal herself. She can't do it alone; there's been too much damage done. She is giving us an urgent message, communicating with us, in the only way she knows how by showing us how sick she is, and desperately asking for our help and our caring, and for our consideration and healing.

Let's be wise enough to listen. Let's consciously care and take positive action. Let's be a lot more respectful of Mother Nature. Let's all help to heal the Earth.

Nineteen

Playing and Procreating

Once upon a time when the Earth was being born, she seeded and co-created herself with the help of the wind and the sun and the rain. Slowly, she birthed herself and grew into a beautiful garden.

Then we came along, to be her children that she blessed with her love. She gave us our home — her home — a beautiful, abundant, healthy place to live. As we grew up, we did some terrible things to her. We disrespected our Mother Earth.

Let's stop playing with destruction and start getting serious about reconstruction.

Now we're co-creators with her, along with the wind and the sun and the rain. We have the awesome power and choice to either re-create a beautiful garden on Earth or to procreate a devastated land.

Together — you and me, all of us — we're creating and procreating our Earth. Let's rebirth her by helping her to heal and to grow herself into the beautiful garden she once was. Let's sow the seeds of caring for her with love, and plant a place of healthy abundance and harmony.

Twenty

Imagine That...
A World View

When my daughter, Jaime, was ten, she came home from school one day and told me about a writing contest that she was thinking about entering. The theme of the contest was "Imagine that..." She asked me for some ideas to help her get started. I thought for a few minutes, then said, "Imagine that the world is a peaceful, happy, beautiful place to live."

This thought stayed on my mind as I imagined that the world really could be a peaceful, happy, beautiful place to live, and that we could make it happen. I thought about what I could do, and as that thought grew, budded, and blossomed, I C.A.R.E. was conceived and born. My daughter had provided the original idea and inspiration.

Being a philosopher at heart, I tend to philosophize from time to time and can even get a little preachy every now and then. I truly believe that we have the power within ourselves to create a beautiful, healthy place to live, right here, right now, and for the future.

We can all help to shape our world simply through our thoughts and the little things we do every day, as well as the large things we do. There are so many ways we can help to heal the Earth, to respect her and care for her in loving, honoring ways, to nurture her and return her to vitality and vibrancy. We have the power to shape and create what our world is now and what it will become.

Think seriously about the kind of place you want to live in now and in the future. Begin creating it now, so that your children and their children are born into a world of beauty — a paradise, a Garden of Eden — a healthy place filled with harmony and joy, peace and love. Do whatever you can, whenever and wherever you can, to help heal our planet. It will make a world of difference.

Be nice to the Earth. Enjoy the Earth. Appreciate her. Respect her, and help to heal our planet now. It's our home. It's where we live in the present, and where we'll live in the future.

You can create the world any way you want to with your actions and through your ideas, dreams, imagination, thoughts, inspiration, and perhaps a bit of perspiration.

Imagine that!!

Part V

Garden Glimpses and Tree Tales

Life is better than beans.

Do love-ins.

Dig in the dirt, plant with care, and let your bloomers be joyful.

Grow babies in the carrot patch.

Get into flower power.

Splash and play. Run through the sprinklers.

Hug and heal some special trees.

Listen for the loving lure.

Grow a jungle in your house and get personal with your plants.

Twenty-One

Plant With Care

When I was four years old, I grew my first garden. I cleared a small area and surrounded it with stones. It was like a ritual and this was my sacred site. I dug through the dirt with a spoon and planted watermelon seeds in the back yard.

I caressed each seed with both my hands and kissed them tenderly before I gently put them into the Earth and covered them over with dirt, which I patted in lovingly. I made sure to plant them in a place that would get a lot of sunlight.

I didn't tell anyone about it, because this was my special secret, my special garden. I watered the seeds every day and talked to them, telling them how much I loved them. I prayed for them, asking them to grow.

One morning I went outside and there was a little, green spike coming up out of the Earth. It was the most joyful day of my life. The Earth had given birth, and had also given me a special, magical gift — a garden.

Twenty-Two

Better Than Beans

When I was in fifth grade, one of our class projects was to grow an indoor bean garden, and then to write a report on it. We put dirt into a plastic cup, planted lima beans and placed the cups by the window.

The cups had our name on them. We each had to water our bean stalk every day and take care of it, making sure that it was standing up straight, and gently adding ties to the stake as our plant became taller.

Some of us didn't need our names on the cup because we *knew* which bean was ours. We had a special connection and bond with our bean that came from caring for it and loving it, like a mother with a child. Our bean was our "baby."

We had a lot of fun with the "My bean is better than your bean" bit, and the "My bean is bigger than yours." Nice, friendly competition that showed our immense pride in what we grew from the Earth.

Growing my beans and watching them get bigger every day helped me realize that I could co-create with the Earth — that the Earth and I could grow things together — that I could give to the Earth, and that the Earth would respond in a similar manner and give to me.

This was a lesson that wasn't taught in the books; it was learned from the heart, by doing and growing. While it was only a few beans, it was much more than that. It was better than beans.

Twenty-Three

"Love-ins"

I grew up in the sixties when "love-ins" were very popular. A group of people (we were called hippies) would gather to share love with each other and with the world. Our purpose was to promote peace. If you're a baby boomer, I'm sure you remember them.

Love-ins are still in style. You can do "love-ins" with the Earth. It promotes peace, joy, and harmony, both within your heart and all around you, and you're gathering together with your friends — the flowers.

I "love-in" my flowers when I plant them. I do this by holding them tenderly and with great care as I'm putting them into the Earth, then gently patting in the soil around them. I talk to them as I'm planting them, welcoming them home into my garden, into the Earth, and thanking them for wanting to be part of my garden.

My flowers are my special friends. They promote a lot of peace in my garden, happiness in my heart, and harmony with the world.

The Earth welcomes the plants and seeds into her

womb and nourishes them with the warmth of her soil, and with the sunshine and rain, taking care of them after they're born. I whisper to them as I watch them open up and grow. I nurture them with love.

The seeds we plant now, both in the ground and in our children's minds, are the flowers that will be our baby boomers, and bloomers, of the future.

Let's "love-in" our children into the garden of Earth; they're the future caregivers to Earth. Through our love and care now, let's give them a beautiful Earth to live on, and to love in.

Twenty-Four

Joyful Bloomers

Wrist-deep in dirt while I was planting little lavender impatiens, I noticed that as soon as I "loved-in" my plants, the buds started to open up immediately.

Within ten minutes of planting them, the buds burst open, blooming into beautiful flowers, vibrant and jubilant with joy. It seemed that my impatiens were impatient to grow. It was as if they were singing in the sunshine, happy to be alive, to be set free to grow in the Earth.

The first time this occurred, I thought it was just my imagination, but I watched this happen over and over again with each plant. Perhaps they were a fast-blooming flower, but I think that being loved-in had something to do with it too.

Flowers, bushes, and trees — all things in nature and in life — respond to love. The Earth responds to love. Let's all plant joyful bloomers.

Twenty-Five

Digging in the Dirt

Let's roll up our sleeves and get our hands dirty by planting and playing in the mud. Let's seed the soil with flowers, bushes, and trees. Let's all plant the Earth with gardens. Let's make our Earth beautiful, and heal her with harmony.

Planting my garden gives me a good, grown-up excuse to play in the dirt. I love getting my hands into the dirt and running my fingers through it. It feels wonderfully silky and smooth to my touch. I love the feel of soft, warm mud oozing through my fingers.

It's so much fun to plant flowers in the Earth and look at what you get for your efforts — a beautiful garden you can enjoy, and one that others will enjoy too when they walk by and see it.

When people walk past my garden, they stop to admire the flowers. A few hours or days later, they walk by again but this time they have their friends or family with them. Some people even come back with a camera to take pictures.

Every year I always win first place in the "Prettiest Patio/Best Balcony" contest sponsored by the managers of my apartment complex.

But I don't grow my garden to win prizes. I grow it because it gives me joy, because it also gives enjoyment and pleasure to other people, and because it's very happy and healing for the Earth.

I win more than the prettiest patio award. I win the best prize of all — my garden.

Twenty-Six

Flower Power

I often go outside and meditate in my garden. It's filled with more than flowers; there's a real, palpable feeling of harmony and peace vibrating in tune with nature and within the Earth. My garden radiates an aura of joy and happiness. This feeling emanates both from within me and from the flowers.

Your garden, and what you grow in it, is an expression of what's inside you and what you portray on the outside. It shows what's inside your heart and shares your soul with the Earth. The flowers you choose to plant in your garden become your special friends, sharing their soul with yours.

Every flower in a garden has its own essence, its own life-force and vibration. The flowers share with you the special treasures and radiance of who they are. They show you on the outside what is deep within them. They show you their soul.

Every garden is beautiful in its own special, unique, magical way, and brings joy and harmony, both to you, the garden grower, and to the Earth.

Twenty-Seven

Jungle Joy

When people walk into my house, the first thing they say is, "It looks like a jungle in here," because I have so many plants growing inside. Little do they know how close they are to the truth.

I occasionally take showers with my plants to create humidity and health for them. I place them in the bathroom and share the steam from the shower with them to create a rain forest atmosphere. Perhaps I'm a shaman at heart and in spirit.

My indoor garden gives me a lot of pleasure in the winter when it's cold and dreary outside, and my outdoor garden goes within itself to sleep — to dream about the warmth and light of Spring — to rejuvenate and transform itself, preparing to bud and bloom again when the sun and rain calls it forth and gives it life anew.

I talk to all my plants and touch them. I send them feelings of good cheer, and health and harmony. I send love vibrations from my heart to them in my thoughts and receive good vibes from them in return.

Indoor plants give you a lot of happiness and joy.

They create an atmosphere and ambiance of vibrancy and harmony in your home, and the greenness is very healing, both for your visual senses and for your spirit. They help to create fresh air for you to breathe.

If you can't grow a garden outdoors — maybe you don't have the space or whatever — you can always grow one inside.

Twenty-Eight

The Carrot Patch

My youngest daughter's first garden was a carrot patch that she and I planted from seed.

She'd toddle out to her garden every day, carrying her favorite stuffed animal who, by some strange coincidence, was named "Carrot."

She'd sit by her garden, singing and talking to it. She lavished all her love and attention on the carrots that she knew were growing in the Earth. She knew that the Earth was magic, and she believed that the seeds were alive.

Jaime grew babies in her garden. Two little preemies, twins, were born first. They were absolutely beautiful, and were the pride of her sweet, little heart.

The next year we planted the proverbial cabbage patch, and many more babies were born.

Not surprisingly, now that Jaime is grown up, her favorite vegetable is carrots.

Twenty-Nine

Loving Lure

When my daughters were little, I gave them parts of my garden for them to grow together with me, and to show them how to care about and for the Earth.

We went to the garden center and I let them choose their own flowers. I taught them how to listen for the "loving lure," to know which plants wanted to come home with them and be in their garden. I told them that the plants would call to them, saying, "I'm over here, come and find me."

And when they had followed the lure from the flowers to where they were in the garden center and found the plants that had called to them, they would know which ones were special, which ones were theirs that wanted to come home with them, by gently touching them and sensing their energy vibrations.

When we got home with their flowers and were in the garden ready to plant them, I showed them how to connect more deeply with their plants, how to open their heart to share their love with the flowers, and to receive the love emanating and radiating from the flowers to them.

I told them that flowers are very special friends, with very special feelings, and that the flowers would share their feelings with them and give them happiness and joy in their hearts. Then I showed them how to love-in their flowers into the Earth.

They had as much fun as I did, if not more, digging in the dirt, planting their flowers, and watching them grow.

By including them in growing gardens, they responded by growing to care for the Earth as much as I do.

Thirty

Splash Bash

Have fun. Play. The Earth loves to hear your laughter. She is our mother and we are her children. Even though you're an adult now, get back into the role of being a child again every now and then. Experience the child-like wonder and joy of being completely carefree and happy.

I had one of the happiest and most hilarious moments in my life with my daughter Jaime when she and I were playing in the sprinklers. I still laugh about it every time I think of it.

We lived in a large apartment complex and during the summer, the grounds were watered with the kind of sprinklers that go from side-to-side in semi-circles. Jaime and I would run through the sprinklers together.

The rules of the game were not to get caught in the spray. The timing on this had to be perfect, because we only had a few seconds before the sprinkler would arc back. We got to be quite good at it, but every once in a while, we'd get all wet.

At first, we'd hold hands and run together

through the dry space between the spray. Then we thought it would be more fun to keep score, to see who could run through the sprinklers the most without being caught.

We decided to take turns. She'd run through first and then I'd run through. One time she got impatient waiting for me to run through and decided to run through a second time. As I mentioned, we were both quite proficient at this and our timing was usually perfect.

However, this time, we both ran through from opposite sides at the same time and met each other smack dab in the middle, knocking each other over into the grass and getting soaking wet.

I just sat there and was laughing so hard that I couldn't get up, but she got up immediately and stood to the side, humiliated, glaring at me. Actually, I was hysterical with laughter and rolled around in the grass.

She didn't think it was funny at all, but she did seem to be concerned about my well-being and my state of mind. Eventually, a few minutes later, she took pity on me and helped me up, then stomped home not walking with me.

The next day she could see the humor in the situation and we decided to make the game even more interesting and challenging. We'd run through from opposite sides at the same time, keeping clear of one another, darting through the dry space and avoiding the spray.

Thirty-One

Have You Hugged a Tree Today?

Remember the very popular bumper sticker that almost everyone had on their car that read, "Have you hugged your kid today?" I have a question for you. "Have you hugged a tree with your kid today?"

Jaime and I used to walk around hugging trees together (when we weren't running through sprinklers, or should I say running into one another?).

When we first met Bushy, she was a limp, almost lifeless, evergreen tree that was more brown than green. Jaime and I decided that this tree definitely needed lots of hugging and a little help from us. Bushy grew into a tall, magnificent tree with daily hugs, large doses of healing and happy thoughts, and lots of love.

When we first saw Willow, we couldn't believe that a tree could get that big around. It took both of us at the same time to hug her, stretching our arms around her as far as we could reach, with our fingers barely touching. It was truly awesome to feel the incredible energy that this tree had. It was so alive and vibrant.

Hugging trees is very helpful and healing, both for you and the tree. Trees respond to your touch in the same way that your children respond to loving hugs. Hug a tree with your kid today. And don't forget to hug your kid.

Thirty-Two

Special Trees

When I was a little girl, I had a special tree that I'd talk to every day. I'd share my secrets with the tree and the tree would listen to my thoughts and feelings, then whisper back to me. This tree became my best friend. My parents told me that the tree couldn't really talk, but I didn't believe them; I knew better.

As I grew up, I continued to communicate with trees, and to have a unique relationship with them.

There is a tree in my front yard that I named Twister because it looks like a tornado. Skinny like a spiral at the bottom, then filling out at the top. It leans way over to one side, like it's going to fall and has no visible means of support.

I'm usually fairly graceful and co-ordinated, but one time I tripped and was headed down hard. Twister was nearby, but was just out of my reach, just an inch or two, too far away to touch or grab onto to help me break my fall.

I swear to you that this tree reached out and caught me, or maybe it was the tree deva. The tree moved and grabbed my hand, gently easing my fall, and letting me down slowly.

There is another special tree in the forest preserve that is close to my home. I call this tree Clarity. I go there often during the summer to relax or when I want to simply be in nature, and to commune with the Earth. It's located in a quiet, private place, in a circular clearing where the sunshine is bright and the wind whispers softly through the leaves.

Sometimes I'll bring a book to read, or my journal to write in or to reflect on the thoughts and feelings I've previously written. Other times, I'll scribble notes for a book I'm in the process of writing. I feel wonderfully inspired there.

It's a huge, old, comfortable tree, perfect for sitting under and snuggling up to when I want to meditate, to ponder problems, to feel happy and peaceful when I'm sad or stressed out. I always feel very comforted and refreshed when I visit Clarity.

Trees are very much alive, and are very aware, and can be your special friends.

Part VI

More Than Magical

Breathe the Earth inside you.

Smile at the sun and sing in the sunshine.

Promote peace; create good vibrations.

Whisper your wishes to the wind.

Bless the Earth and the entire world with love.

Thirty-Three

Breathe

Breathe the fresh air.

Breathe the beautiful scent and aroma of the Earth into your lungs.

Feel it flow through you, revitalizing you and nourishing you, giving you life and energy.

Breathe in the beauty and joy and harmony of the Earth around you.

Breathe out your love and healing thoughts to the Earth, sharing your spirit with the Earth.

Enjoy being and breathing on this beautiful Earth.

Simply breathe.

Thirty-Four

Smile at the Sun

The sun gives light and life to the Earth. The light is more than magical; it's one of the sources that powers the Earth with energy and feeds her soul. The sun nourishes and nurtures the Earth; it helps to grow the grass, the flowers, and the trees.

The sun also gives us light and helps to keep us alive. We're not that much different than the Earth, and we need the sun as much as she does. Take a moment every now and then to appreciate the light, and to be grateful.

Sunshine feels warm and wonderful on your face and body. The sun revitalizes and rejuvenates us. The light offers us health and harmony; it nourishes our bodies and uplifts our spirits. Let the light from the sun nurture your heart and grow your mind.

Open up your soul to the sun, and experience what the Earth experiences in the light from the sun. Power yourself with the sun's inherent energy.

Smile at the sun. Laugh in the sunshine. Feel joy and harmony in your heart. Sing and dance in the rays of light. It's a happy thing to do and is very healing, both for you and the Earth.

Thirty-Five

Promote Peace

Promoting peace, both actively in your actions and passively in your thoughts, creates a corresponding vibration of energy in the Earth.

The energies of war and hate have created negative, harmful impressions and imprints in the energy fields of the Earth. Simply by thinking and acting peacefully, and sending thoughts of harmony to the Earth, we can help to heal these negative energies in a powerful, positive way.

We can grow peace. By planting the Earth with gardens and trees in areas that have been torn apart by war and destruction, we can heal the wounds of war and soothe the scars of hate. We can replenish and restore the land with love, as well as with flowers and trees.

One flower in a barren wasteland of war can grow into a beautiful meadow of flowers. Just one flower is all it takes; just one thought of peace and harmony begins to grow, seeds itself, and reproduces.

The Earth responds in like manner to the energy we put forth. If we all simply think peace and promote peace in our actions, the world will become a peaceful, harmonious place to live.

Love is ever so much more powerful than hate. Peace is stronger than war. Love the Earth, promote peace, and think happy, healing thoughts.

This is such a little, easy thing for us to do and yet it can accomplish so much.

Let's all sow the seeds of peace and reap a healthy harvest of harmony.

Thirty-Six

Whisper to the Wind

One of the most positive and joyful ways to heal the Earth is to radiate and send vibrations of love and harmony to the Earth.

Our thoughts are heard, loudly and clearly, and influence the energies of the Earth in a tremendously powerful way.

Go outside and listen to the wind as it softly whispers. Feel the gentle breeze on your body and the soft caress of its touch. Breathe with the wind and become one with the wind; consciously being and breathing with it.

As you tune into the energies of the wind and connect with the vibrations of the Earth, harmonize your heart and soul with thoughts of love, peace, joy, and harmony.

Whisper happy, healing thoughts into the wind. Let the wind carry your wishes to bless the Earth, and to reach into the furthermost corners of the world.

Part VII

Nature Spirits and Shamans

Make friends with the flower faeries. Get to know the devas, and invite overlighting angels into your garden.

Commune with nature in a real way.

Be a home-grown shaman — a person of Earth wisdom and healing.

Dream a more-than-magical dream and make it come to life.

Thirty-Seven

Make Friends With the Flower Faeries

Believe it or not, flower faeries and other nature spirits are real. They help to grow your garden and to care for all the flowers, and for everything in nature that grows on the Earth. They're much more than a "fairy" tale.

Flowers, vegetables, bushes, plants, and trees need more than sunshine, rain, love, and the Earth to grow. By learning how to talk to nature, to commune with nature, and especially by learning how to listen, we can attune ourselves into the world of nature and its subtle energies.

We can communicate with the flower faeries and other nature spirits who are the caregivers and co-creators of our Earth. We can share our essence and be in harmony with them. We can help them to grow our gardens.

If you're tuned into the flowers, you can sense their presence and sometimes catch a glimpse of the flower faeries shimmering in the sunshine, or see them dancing on the grass or gliding gracefully through the air. You might see them in a sparkling dewdrop on a flower, or in a sprinkle of rain on a leaf. Sometimes you can hear them singing and laughing in the gentle, quiet breeze.

Flower faeries, overlight angels, elves, nature spirits, devas, and many other elementals are the growers, gardeners, protectors, and keepers of the plant kingdom on Earth.

They desire our help and companionship. We can offer them many things, and they can offer us, and the Earth, so much more. We can learn how to work in harmony with them to grow our gardens. They know best where to plant your garden, and what to plant in it. They're more than happy and willing to offer their advice and share their knowledge.

Learning how to communicate with flower faeries and other nature spirits requires respect, sincerity, and a commitment to work with them. Begin by meditating in your garden, or in any natural setting. Open your mind and your heart, and express your desire to work in harmony with them.

Silently speak to them, and listen with more than your ears; listen with your heart. They'll begin to communicate with you in your thoughts and feelings. Be receptive to any kind of loving response that you receive, and **believe** that it isn't just your imagination. **Know** that this is real.

When they see that you are serious, and that you love and care for the Earth, they will appear or make themselves known to you.

Thirty-Eight

Shaman's Spirit

Shamans are the healers and wise people of Native American Indians and other indigenous people from around the world who are in touch with and in tune with the energies of the Earth. They know how to walk through and weave together the energies of nature and the Earth with the world around them.

Their lives are filled with a rich tapestry of natural knowledge which they share in helping others. They know the healing properties of plants and how to use them by asking permission and requesting help from the plant's spirit.

They, and their people, practice a natural lifestyle, living in harmony and cooperation with the Earth by respecting the land which gives them life — Mother Earth.

Their philosophies are deeply profound and very Earth-honoring. To tell you the many ways they heal the Earth would take volumes, and volumes have been written about them.

Within the scope of this brief chapter, and to oversimplify their beliefs, they hold true to the thought that *the world is as you dream it.*

We can learn a lot from them, from the seemingly simple way they live. It's a much healthier and a more Earth-honoring lifestyle than most of us practice. Perhaps if we subscribe to their natural wisdom, and we all start dreaming about a healthy Earth, we can help to make it happen.

There are many "home-grown" shamans right here, maybe living next door to you. We're all shamans in spirit — magical, intuitive, knowing people — on the inside.

Let's share the dream about a healthy, beautiful Earth and help to bring it forth, first in our dreams and then in reality. We have the inherent power to make our dreams come true.

Part VIII

Earth Exercises and Explorations

The Earth is alive. Be at one with her.
Experience her heartbeat and breath.

Tune into the energies of nature to know the secrets and mysteries of all living things. Experience their essence and life-force.

Thirty-Nine

The Earth is Alive

The Earth is a living, breathing, beautiful, vibrant being. The energy of the Earth is as palpable as a heartbeat, as real as a breath. The Earth has a soul — a spiritual awareness — as well as a physical consciousness.

The following Earth-Energy Exercise is designed to help you connect with the Earth, to help you realize and to really know that the Earth is alive.

This exercise is a meditation excerpted from my book, *Images and Inner Journeys*. Read through the meditation first to see what it says and then adapt it into an awareness exploration if you feel comfortable laying on the Earth.

If you feel silly laying on the grass — maybe you feel that you're too old for this now, or that this is beneath you, or you think that if anyone sees you, they'll think that you're either crazy or you've collapsed — then just imagine in your mind that you're actually doing this meditation. At the very least, do this outside.

If you're a runner or a jogger, or a power-walker

or simply a sidewalk stroller, go for the complete meditation, otherwise skip to the part about laying on the ground.

It's a beautiful, sunny day and you're outside, running in a wide-open, grassy expanse of Earth, totally enjoying your physical exercise and the harmony you feel with your body. The blueness of the sky and the greenness of the grass surrounds you and envelops you.

It's just you and the sky and the Earth. You feel a wonderful sense of total freedom all around you as you experience complete harmony with the sky and the air, and with the Earth and the grass. Everything around you and within you is vibrantly alive, pulsing with life, and you feel more energized than you've ever felt before.

You're very aware of the rhythm of your pace, your breathing and heartbeat, and how your pace matches the energies within you and the vibrations of everything around you. You feel the energies of the Earth vibrating in rhythm with your pace, in rhythm with the energies inside your physical body. You're completely focused on and tuned into this special feeling of being at one with yourself, and at the same time, being at one with nature and in harmony with the Earth.

You've been running for several miles, experiencing the joy of your freedom and movement, and your energy and the exhilaration of your physical exercise, but now you begin to slow down. Tapering off to a walk and then stopping to rest, you lie in the soft green grass, feeling your heart beat and being aware of your breathing.

Looking at the bright blueness of the cloudless sky, smelling the fresh scent of the green grass, and breathing *in the pure, clean air, you again sense the harmonies all around you and within you. You sense that your inner energy is very similar to the energy within the Earth.*

A gentle breeze is blowing, refreshing you. You become even more aware of how the vibrations of everything around you matches your own inner vibrations, and this realization inspires within you a deeper feeling of harmony and oneness with nature, a feeling of being truly connected with the Earth.

You feel a strong sense of energy and vitality coming up from the Earth, almost like a heartbeat. At first you think that it's your heart beating from the long run, but soon you realize it's more than that. You're feeling the energy of the Earth beneath you. The Earth feels as if it's alive. It has a heartbeat and breath, just like you.

Tuning in even more to the vibrant energies of the Earth, you begin to recognize that the Earth is a living, breathing being. Feeling the Earth breathe in rhythm with your breathing, and sensing its essence — its heartbeat — pulsing from within, in harmony with your heartbeat, you feel completely connected to the energy of the Earth.

Feeling grounded and centered within yourself, you simultaneously sense and feel the life-force and energy of the Earth beneath you — breathing, vibrant, and very much alive, just like you.

Breathe, and be at one with the Earth.

Forty

Earth Energies

Everything in nature is alive and has a voice. All we need to do is to tune in and listen to what nature has to say. Experiencing the energies of nature is very magical and can help to make you more aware of the life-force within all living things. The Earth will share her secrets and the mysteries of her magic if you'll listen to her.

In the following Earth-Awareness experiences, you'll be exploring two of the life-forces and energies within nature by combining your awareness with a leaf and a pebble to help you understand their individual energy essences by sensing and obtaining information about them. Everything you experience will help you to open up your awareness and perceptions of nature, and to understand how you are connected with nature and with the Earth.

This is easy to do. In fact, it's so easy that even a baby can do it. Have you ever noticed how a baby explores the world around him? He studies everything he finds thoroughly and with utter fascination. He focuses his complete attention on the object and uses all five physical senses to obtain direct knowing about it. By doing this, the baby learns how the object fits into his world and what purposes it serves. I would even venture to say that he also understands the inner energies as well as the outer vibrations of the object.

Every baby has explored a leaf and truly knows and understands what nature is really like; you've probably done it too but have forgotten about it. Ask any mother or turn a crawling baby loose in the back yard and watch him for five minutes or less. He'll go straight for the leaf and study it thoroughly before he puts it in his mouth. So you're actually rediscovering something you already know everything about.

Pick a leaf from a plant, bush, or tree, but not just any leaf. Look at the leaves and choose one that you feel drawn to, one that you sense would be right. Maybe touch several of them to become aware of their vibes.

Before you pick the leaf, ask its permission. You may think this is silly or strange, but you'll understand why after you explore and experience its energy essence.

In your mind, imagine that you're talking to the leaf and ask permission to take it from the tree or plant. Explain your reasons; tell it why you want it. Tell the leaf that you want to know more about its essence and that you want to understand what the energies in nature are really like.

Listen quietly and you'll become aware of some type of response or feeling from the leaf that will indicate whether or not you can pick it. Respect the answer that comes to you. If the leaf is willing to participate, you'll get a sense that it's okay to use it. Be sure to say thank you. You are talking to a living thing that has feelings.

Gently take it from the bush or tree. When you have the leaf in your hand, study it completely and thoroughly. Really see what it looks like. View it with all the curiosity and inquisitiveness of something you're discovering for the very first time.

Use all your physical senses to find out everything you can about it. Touch the leaf; caress it gently, feel its texture. Sense the energy that flows within it and its life-force that emanates and radiates from its inner essence to the aura around it. Taste it; take a small bite of it or break it open and lick it. Smell it; really breathe in its scent. Hold it up to your ear and listen carefully to it, to the quiet sounds it makes.

After you've gathered this outer information, hold the leaf gently in your hand. Touching or holding it will help you tune into the vibrations of energy that are within it and are emitted from it. The impressions you receive through your physical sense of touching and your inner sense of feeling will help you to become clearer and more aware of the energy within it.

While holding it gently in your hand, either between your thumb and forefinger, or by folding your fingers around it, or cupping it in the palm of your hand and placing your other hand over it, close your eyes, enter a meditative frame of mind and experience the energy essence and the life within this leaf.

Go inside its energies and completely experience being inside the leaf; gather all the information you can about it. Sense its vibrations with your mind, your heart, and your soul.

Take a journey — a magical mind trip — through the inner workings and feelings and energy vibrations of this leaf. Be the leaf. Explore and experience the life-force and energy inside the leaf. Take your time with this; you'll be amazed at what this leaf has to say to you and can show you.

When you're done, thank the leaf, sprinkle it with water and return it to the Earth so that it's touching the plant or tree where it came from. If you'd like, stay outside for a while to commune with nature.

* * * * * *

To become aware of the difference in energy vibrations between the leaf and other living things in nature, do the same thing with a pebble. Even a stone has its energy essence and can show you many magical things. Before you pick it up from the ground, ask the stone if you can move it, promising to return it when you're through.

Explore it with all your physical and inner senses to experience what it's really like to be this stone, to be inside its energies. It's more alive than you might think it is. Explore and discover the inner vibrations and the energy that this rock emits. When you're done, thank the stone and return it to the Earth.

By doing these awareness-expanding exercises, you're exploring and experiencing the inner energy and the life-force that exists in everything in nature, and in the Earth as well. This helps you to achieve an understanding of their inter-relationship, and offers you a direct knowing of their inner essence so that you become more aware that everything in nature, and the Earth herself, is just as alive and aware as you are.

This awareness helps you to tune into nature and teaches you how to communicate with nature. It helps you to become much more respectful of Earth energies, and all the life energies in nature, so that you'll know, on a deep, inner, intuitive level, how to honor and heal the Earth.

If you want to further explore and to better understand the soul of the Earth and the energies of nature, here are a few more exercises to do:

1. Explore and experience the energy essence of sunshine, rain, trees, clouds, flowers, a rainbow, the air you breathe, etc., by going inside their life-force.

2. Listen to the sound of a babbling brook or a waterfall as it sings its song to you. Sit beneath a tree and meditate. Listen to the secrets of nature that it shares with you. Communicate with the devas and the flower faeries who grow your garden. Watch the sunrise, and become part of it, to discover the soul of the sun.

3. Play with the clouds. Look up at the puffy white clouds in the sky and create shapes with them. Or make one disappear and re-appear somewhere else in the sky. Imagine that you're a cloud. Merge your awareness with the cloud and float through the sky. If it's a rainy day, ask the clouds to stop raining

or move them along. Or simply enjoy them as they are. If it's a sunny day, ask the clouds to rain and then ask the sun to create a rainbow.

4. Sit quietly on the ground, with an open heart and a receptive frame of mind, and go inside the energies of the Earth to see what the Earth shows you and to understand what the Earth is all about.

5. Connect yourself with the energies of the Earth in a spiritual, loving, harmonious way. Commune with the essence of the Earth by intertwining your soul with hers. Ask the Earth what you can do to honor and heal her. Listen with both your mind and your heart, and she will speak to you and share her soul with you.

Part IX

Take Action.
Do Something!

Stand up on your soapbox.

Make your thoughts matter.

Show your kids that you care and let them care too. Plant fertile seeds in the Earth and in their minds.

Get helping hands together and gather a clean-up crew.

Forty-One

Soapbox Stand

There's this little soapbox that I like to stand on from time to time. It's where I throw in my two cents for whatever it's worth when there's something that I truly believe in and feel very strongly about.

What kind of world do you want to live in, and what are you doing about it? This brings me to my soapbox stand — to one of the things I want to say about caring for the Earth.

Stand up on your soapbox (literally and figuratively) and talk to people about the real need now to honor and heal the Earth, to cleanse and purify her of the toxins and wastes we are dumping on her and in her. Talk to your neighbors and friends. Get preachy and teachy.

Talking to people can be a lot of fun and you get to meet interesting people and become aware of their ideas, to listen to what they're doing and to hear about how they feel about the Earth. If they're not doing anything, then maybe you can inspire them to become involved — to do something to help.

The Earth is alive and is just sick about what

we've been doing to her. If we're not careful, and we don't take care of her, she might just dry up and die. She needs her resources to sustain herself and to take care of us. Let's give back what she's given to us, what we've taken from her.

Please, I beg of you, as an environmentalist, as a mother and soon-to-be grandmother, and as someone who simply cares about the Earth, let's take good care of her. Let's respect her and restore her to a state of health and harmony.

Her life depends on us, and our life depends on her. We need her and she needs us. Let's do more than verbalize and pay lip service. Let's actualize and really make things happen. Let's get involved; let's give more and take less, and most of all, let's CARE. Let's honor and heal the Earth in many happy ways.

Forty-Two

Make it Matter

Make it matter and make it happen. While thoughts appear to be illusionary and intangible, zipping in and out of your mind, in reality thoughts are tangible things. They manifest and they do more than matter — they turn into matter.

Many years ago, when I was working part-time at the local library, two caring people there had instituted a recycling program for employees. The bins were kept inside, in the employee lounge.

When I left the library, there was no place that I knew of to recycle my milk cartons, newspapers, and aluminum cans, so I would make a special trip over there once a week. Then I decided that I'd like to be able to recycle when I tossed out my trash.

It also occurred to me that many other people would recycle if it was easy for them to do. Since I lived in an apartment, I started calling the manager and sending him letters, requesting a recycling center for the complex.

In addition, I called the waste management company that picked up our garbage and found out that recycling pick-up was the same price as regular garbage collection, so I included that information in my letters to the manager.

I kept after him with phone calls and letters, and one day I walked outside to the dumpster and saw recycling bins there. I was so happy that I ran inside to call him immediately to thank him.

A few letters and phone calls were all the energy and effort I put into this and now 300 families who live in my apartment complex recycle. It was so easy to accomplish. I received so much joy from seeing the recycling bins in place and knowing that I was helping to honor and heal the Earth.

It all started with an intangible idea, a little thought that grew in my mind and blossomed into being. Making it matter and making it happen works like that.

Forty-Three

Kids Care

Get your kids involved. Show them that you care about the Earth and let them care too. The benefits to this are plentiful and far-reaching. It brings you and your children closer together. By showing and teaching them — by letting them help you — they learn to honor and respect the Earth. Being actively involved in growing a garden, in both the planting and caring for it, inspires them as they grow to continue caring for the Earth.

You'll be planting seeds for the future of the Earth in the garden of your children's minds. The Earth is a fertile planting ground; your children's minds are ever so much more fertile and receptive. Grow your kids in a garden of love.

It's never too late or too early to start, and the sooner the better. If your children are very young, talk to them about caring for the Earth, and let them see how much you care.

If you plant a garden, tell them that a few of the flowers belong to them and point them out. Let that be their special space. Allow them to gently touch the flowers and help to water them. This invites them to form a more loving bond with you and inspires a loving, caring connection with the Earth.

Sow the seeds of the future with your children in their minds, hearts, and souls. They are the future caregivers and gardeners of the Earth. Plant beautiful thoughts in their mind; watch them bud and blossom and grow in many beautiful ways.

Forty-Four

Clean-up Crew

You keep your house clean; let's also keep the Earth clean. Most of us clean on Saturdays, and we've been doing this all our life. Even though cleaning seems like a chore, we're rewarded for our efforts. We enjoy living in a clean house, and the Earth enjoys a clean environment.

Family Fun

Remember the Saturday chores you used to do when you were younger? Maybe once a month, for an hour or so, you and your kids could do ecology chores together by helping to clean up the Earth and the environment. Walk around the neighborhood and pick up the litter. Make it an enjoyable experience, not a chore. Turn it into a fun, family event — a day outside to enjoy and appreciate nature and a clean environment.

Offer Earth-oriented prizes like a picnic lunch in the park or a forest preserve, followed by a volleyball or badminton game, or simply offer praises to the one who picks up the most trash.

Maybe other neighborhood kids, and some adults, will see what you're doing and offer to help and join in with you.

If the reverse happens, and sometimes, sadly, it might, and your kid's friends make fun of them, advise your kids to stand up proudly and say, "I'm cleaning up the Earth. What are you doing to help?"

Do age-appropriate clean-ups. This idea works best with younger children, but the suggestion works equally well with older kids.

School Stuff

Grow your clean-up crew by involving your children's school in your efforts. Begin a group clean-up movement by speaking up at PTA meetings. Or have your kids ask their teachers what they can do as a class to help clean up the Earth and the environment.

Maybe they could do a clean-up of the school grounds on a Saturday, followed by planting a tree in front of the school or a garden of flowers nestled close to the building.

Increase the scope; make it bigger and better. Maybe the entire school, along with some teachers and parents, could "adopt" a local beach or a lake, or a park to clean up. Then do a fun activity there to celebrate the clean environment. But remember that the real prize, or reward, is a clean Earth and a beautiful area that your community can be proud of.

Community Clean-up

If there's an unused area of land, or an abandoned lot in your neighborhood, find out who owns or manages it, and offer to do a clean-up in exchange for planting a community vegetable garden there, with everyone sharing the planting and tending of the crops. Ask the local garden center to donate the seeds or the plants.

When the crops are ripe, have a harvest festival — a farmer's market — and sell the vegetables. Use the money for next year's crop planting or other environmental projects.

If you don't have kids, or they're grown up and are on their own, call kindergartens or elementary or junior high schools in your area to see what they're doing to help clean up the Earth and what you can volunteer for or sponsor or get involved with.

You'll be doing very wonderful and helpful things for yourself, your kids, your community, and most especially, for the Earth.

Forty-Five

Helping Hands

Combine your energies and efforts with other people in your area to make your community a nicer place to live. Contact local park districts or environmental organizations or your community center to find out what they're doing.

Join in and help; volunteer. You'll have fun doing it, you'll make new friends, and you'll be helping to heal the Earth in a very wonderful way.

If there are no local organizations or programs in your area, start one. Be creative. Implement a recycling program or originate your own environmental organization. Ask your friends and neighbors to become involved, and to help you.

Get a group together of caring, committed people in your community. Arrange a gathering at the town hall, or a similar place, to let other people know what you're doing and what you'd like to achieve. Invite them to attend, to share their ideas, thoughts, and suggestions, and to become actively involved.

Announce this meeting by posting flyers around your community on the library bulletin board, in grocery stores, and in the windows of local retailers and businesses who support your efforts.

Obtain free media coverage. Advertise this event by sending a press release to the local newspaper, and by calling the local TV and radio stations to let them know what you're doing.

There are many ways to show that you care, and to help. If you can't take an active role because your schedule is very busy, do what you can as an individual on a daily basis. Just simply recycle, and send happy, healing thoughts to the Earth. This shows that you care and is incredibly helpful in healing the Earth in more ways than you may be aware of. Little things go a long way.

Part X

Consciously Care

Care about the Earth.

Create a happy, healthy Earth.

Live in a beautiful land of peaceful harmony, and leave a loving legacy.

Forty-Six

Care About the Earth

Just simply care about the Earth. Renew her resources, and respect the Earth. There are so many ways you can help to heal the Earth. As a caring individual, everything you do has a tremendous influence on the Earth.

In whatever way that is happy and joyful and appropriate for you, honor and heal the Earth every day. You can be a wonderful caregiver to the Earth. It is your right and privilege to live on a beautiful land, and it is also your responsibility to take care of it.

Invest your time and energy into honoring and healing the Earth. Get involved. Share your ideas and information with other people. Show that you care in every way that you can, in every moment. Look around you and within your heart. See what you can do to help; see what you can give to the Earth.

There are so many happy, helpful ways to heal the Earth in all the things that you do. Just give it a little thought, some time now and then, and your respect all the time. All it really takes is conscious caring. You and the Earth will be richly rewarded.

What you do and what you give, no matter what it is, or how small or large it is, is a beautiful gift to the Earth, given with your love, through your heart, mind, and soul.

Everything you do matters, whether it's thinking a thought, recycling, planting a garden, hugging a tree, or simply appreciating nature.

You can make a huge difference, and the gifts you give will be treasured by the Earth, shared with and enjoyed by everyone who lives on the Earth.

You are leaving a legacy for your children and your grandchildren, and for all future generations. Give them a healthy Earth. It's the greatest gift you can give. **CARE.**

Part XI

A Garden of Harmony

A very special gift from the Earth to you — a love present from her heart.

Forty-Seven

A Special Gift From the Earth to You

Just as you can help to heal the Earth in many happy, loving ways, especially by planting gardens, the Earth can help to heal you.

Being in a beautiful garden is beneficial for your health. It promotes peace and harmony, both inside your mind and in your body, as well as uplifting and healing your spirit. It's also very effective in reducing stress and in calming anger or other negative emotions.

Being in a garden can help you to meditate, to go within yourself and touch your true nature, to tune into your inner self — to who you really are on the inside. There are so many wonderful things that a garden can do for you.

The following meditation is excerpted from my book, *Images and Inner Journeys,* and is offered here as a love present — a very special gift — from the Earth to you.

This **Garden of Harmony** meditation is written

to be experienced inside your mind — in your imagination — but is ever so much more powerful and healing when you're actually in a garden.

I wrote this meditation outside, sitting in the grass by a waterfall, surrounded by trees and flowers, on a warm, sunny day with a gentle breeze.

As you read through, and then do, this meditation in your mind or outside in nature, open up your imagination; enhance the meditation and add to it all the special things in nature that you resonate with — with the feelings that inspire and bring peace and harmony to you, and with the images that you feel connected to in a happy, healing way.

Change the meditation in any way that you want to, so that it truly reflects what a garden of harmony is to you. Perhaps the most healing place for you in nature is the beach, or the woods.

You may want to wait to read this meditation until you can be outside in a special place in nature where you've been before and truly feel connected to so that you can completely feel the healing energies of nature with every part of you — with your body, mind, and soul — and to experience the vibrations of health and harmony fully with all your physical and spiritual senses.

Imagine yourself in a very beautiful garden. Looking around, you see many beautiful flowers and lush, flowering bushes spread among open, spacious, grassy areas. The fragrance of the flowers is lovely and pleasing, and the purity of their colors is awe-inspiring.

The bushes and flowers move gently in the soft, warm

breeze, creating balance and beauty within the garden and within your mind. The garden emanates a vibrant feeling of energy, radiant and abundant with life and health.

Everything in your garden vibrates in harmony, in tune with nature. It's quiet and peaceful, and the air is clean and pure and refreshing. Breathing in, you sense the oneness of the garden with nature and you sense that same oneness within yourself as you begin to absorb the harmony and the healing energies of the garden within your body, your mind, and your spirit.

The day is filled with warm sunshine and a brilliant blue sky above you. The light and warmth of the sun on your face and body feels wonderful and rejuvenating. The grass beneath your bare feet feels soft and luxuriant.

The healing colors of the blue sky and the green grass surround you, enveloping you with a calm, gentle, peaceful feeling.

The warmth from the sun's rays begin to permeate and radiate through you, filling you with a wonderful feeling of health and harmony. You feel perfectly in tune with nature and with the energies of sunlight.

Within your garden, you feel drawn to a very special place of peace and harmony where you feel most in tune with the healing energies of sunlight and nature all around you. As you enter this special healing place in your garden, you feel completely at peace with yourself and totally in harmony with the beauty and serenity all around you.

In this special healing place, **feel** the vibrations of energy that are both around you and within you. Center in on the warmth and light from the sun. **Feel** the healing energies of sunlight gently vibrating all around you, flowing through you and within you.

Breathe in the sunlight; breathe in the beauty and greenness of the Earth and the blueness of the sky. Breathe in the health and harmony of this garden deeply inside you — into every part of your body, your mind, and your spirit.

Feel your mind, your thoughts and feelings, and your body vibrating in harmony with the light, totally in tune with both your physical and spiritual nature, completely in tune with the peaceful, healing energies of your garden.

Experience and enjoy the perfect health and harmony you feel within yourself — within your body, your mind, and your spirit.

Take all the time you want or need with this, then bring the peace and harmony you feel within every part of you, and the radiant vibrations of light and health you've just experienced, into your conscious mind and let them flow through your thoughts and feelings, and your body over and over again.

Allow this Garden of Harmony to become a special place of healing for you whenever you need it, or if you just want to be in a pleasant place to enjoy serenity and peace of mind.

This garden is a beautiful, loving gift from the Earth to you — a love present from her heart.

Publisher's Note

You can help to grow this book into a garden of books. Share your stories, suggestions, thoughts, ideas, and happy ways that YOU honor and heal the Earth.

Articles published in future books will be paid for, credited with a by-line and a brief bio, if appropriate, and you'll receive two complimentary copies of the book. You'll also be given a nice discount if you want to buy additional copies to give to your friends, or to sell at your classes and lectures if you're a teacher or a speaker.

Share and show that you care. Send your articles — you can send more than one — typed, double-spaced, anywhere from a paragraph up to 3-4 pages, to I C.A.R.E., Attention: Gloria Chadwick, Mystical Mindscapes, 1908 Cambridge Court, Suite 2A, Palatine, IL 60074.

Your articles may be edited for content and clarity. Written permission to use your work is required; please include this with your submission.

All articles received will be acknowledged. Please enclose a SASE.

Recommended Reading List

The following books are ones that I found most helpful and meaningful to me. They're special because the authors are impassioned environmentalists who share their knowledge, and their caring for the well-being of the Earth comes through in their words. You may enjoy reading them too.

Within many of these books, you'll find useful facts and reference and resource lists of other books and organizations that are dedicated to honoring and healing the Earth.

Behaving As If The God In All Life Mattered and *Co-Creative Science*, Machaelle Small Wright, Perelandra

Both books describe the world of nature and the plant, animal, and mineral kingdoms. They show the rhythms of nature and its ecological balance, and encourage us to become partners with nature and conscious caretakers of our Earth. Two of her other books — *Perelandra Garden Workbooks* — offer a complete guide to gardening with devas and nature spirits.

Clearcut, Bill Hunger, Hampton Roads Publishing

A fictional, but very real, novel about the consequences of cutting down and killing the forests.

Deva Handbook: How to Work with Nature's Subtle

Energies, Nathaniel Altman, Destiny Books

Guides us into the realm of the keepers of Earth wisdom and shows us how we can easily learn to communicate with the devas to heal both ourselves and our Earth in a natural and powerful manner. An excellent and useful book, whether you're planting a garden, tuning into nature, or just appreciating the wonders and joys of the Earth.

Elves of Lily Hill Farm, Penny Kelly, Llewellyn Publications

A true story of the author's relationship with the elves who help her grow her grape farm by sharing the secrets and sacredness of nature with her. By listening to the land, she discovered a deeper connection with the Earth and learned how to communicate and work with nature spirits.

Enchantment of the Faerie Realm: Communicate with Nature Spirits & Elementals, Ted Andrews, Llewellyn Publications

A wonderfully delightful book that will reawaken you to the magic of nature and renew your connection with the Earth. Offers practical, in-depth methods for contacting and working with the faerie world. Shows how to recognize the presence of faeries, devas, elves, and other nature spirits.

50 Simple Things You Can Do to Save the Earth, Earth Works Press

This book and their other titles — *50 Simple Things Your Business Can Do to Save the Earth*, *50 Simple Things Kids Can Do to Save the Earth*, and *The*

Recycler's Handbook — offer many useful facts and resource information for recycling, and show how we can all take an active role to make a difference.

Findhorn Garden, The Findhorn Community, Harper Collins

Describes the community's work with devas, and how they grew a bountiful garden on desert-like soil by listening to nature and by planting in harmony with the energies of the Earth.

Images and Inner Journeys, Gloria Chadwick, Mystical Mindscapes

Contains many Earth-oriented meditations in addition to the metaphysical visualizations that can help to connect you with your true spiritual nature.

Listening to Nature, Joseph Cornell, Dawn Publications

Offers observations, anecdotes, and exercises you can do to tune into nature and re-align yourself with the energies of Earth. Several of his other books — *Sharing Nature with Children, Journey to the Heart of Nature,* and *Sharing the Joy of Nature* — are designed to help children explore and experience the many wonders and joys of nature. Parents and teachers may want to read these books and do some of the nature exercises with their children and students.

Magical Gardens, Patricia Monaghan, Llewellyn Publications

Shows how to plant magical gardens to attract angels and flower faeries into your life. In the process, you'll honor the soul of the Earth as you discover that the time you spend in your garden is a sacred time.

Partner Earth: A Spiritual Ecology, Pam Montgomery, Destiny Books

Shows ways to open yourself up to communicate with the spirits of nature, plants, and the Earth. Describes how to promote personal and planetary well-being by developing a relationship with nature.

Psychic Power of Plants, John Whitman, Signet Books

Tells how plants respond to thoughts and feelings, and describes how they communicate with each other and with you.

Real World of Fairies, Dora van Gelder, Quest Books

Tells about the author's experiences with fairies. Describes how to communicate with them, how to help them and allow them to help you. Shows how the world of fairies is filled with lightness and joy as they care for all things in nature.

Sastun: My Apprenticeship with a Maya Healer, Rosita Arvigo, Harper

The true story of the author's journey into the rain forest to learn about the natural healing properties of native plants. Her life is dedicated to the preserving of healing plants, and of caring for the Earth.

Secret Garden, Frances Hodgson Burnett, Dell Publishing

A fictional, yet true-to-life, account of how a little

girl found a secret garden and by working with the Earth, she grew much more than a garden. The garden opened her heart and her soul. This is one of my favorite books. It shows how the Earth offered her a special, sacred gift, and how the Earth gives us more than gardens.

Summer with the Leprechauns, Tanis Helliwell, Blue Dolphin Publishing

In this true story, the author recounts her experiences with the leprechaun who shared a summer cottage with her and taught her many things about the world of nature spirits and how to communicate and work in harmony with them to help heal the Earth.

Talking with Nature, Michael J. Roads, H.J. Kramer

Describes the author's experiences that began when a river talked to him and he listened. The book shares the energies and spirits of trees, plants, birds, and the Earth. In his next book, *Journey Into Nature*, the author goes beyond communicating with nature; he becomes the essence of nature.

To Hear the Angels Sing, Dorothy Maclean, Lindisfarne Press

This wonderful, heart-warming book shares the author's experiences and tells how we can reunite with the angelic realms of nature. Simply by listening with our hearts — with the love of nature that is inherent in all of us — we can tune into the divine in nature and work in harmony with the devic kingdom to help heal our Earth.

Wild Communion: Experiencing Peace in Nature, Ruth Baetz, Hazelden

Describes how to commune with nature in our busy and often hectic lifestyles. A moment or two spent in nature restores and rejuvenates our heart, mind, and soul. This book shows us the gifts that the Earth has to offer us, if we will take the time to tune in.

World Is As You Dream It, John Perkins, Destiny Books

Tells about the native shamans in the rain forests in the Andes and the Amazon, and the author's experiences with them. Offers information about how to help heal the Earth by dreaming the world you want into reality.